Reciprocal Support Plan

Reciprocal Support Plan

How to Create Astounding Financial Activity, Greatly Benefiting
Yourself, Your Neighbors, and Your
City, County, State, and Federal Governments

Frederick Bonamici

Oonah Publishing Company

DESERT HOT SPRINGS, CALIFORNIA

Although the author and publisher have made every effort to ensure the
accuracy and completeness of information contained in this book, we assume
no responsibility for errors, inaccuracies, omissions, or any inconsistency
herein. Any slights of people, places, or organizations are unintentional.

First printing 2005

ISBN 0-9765094-2-3   LCCN 2004118437

**ATTENTION CORPORATIONS, UNIVERSITIES, COLLEGES, AND
PROFESSIONAL ORGANIZATIONS:** Quantity discounts are available on
bulk purchases of this book for educational, gift purposes, or as premiums for
increasing magazine subscriptions or renewals. Special books or book
excerpts can also be created to fit specific needs. For information, please
contact Oonah Publishing Company, 66321 Pierson Blvd.,
Desert Hot Springs, CA 92240-3600; 760-251-9889.

Dedicated to my Godson,
Andrew Joseph Cipolla

Reciprocal Support Plan
Mission Statement

To better the living conditions of the people by making extended use of the people's money in conjunction with the money of city, county, state, and federal governments and to convince local governments, with the help of readers, to install and implement the Reciprocal Support Plan (RSP) immediately.

Table of Contents

Part One—Reciprocal Support Plan at the City/County Level

1 **Chapter One** 5

Setting Up the Reciprocal Support Plan (RSP)

No Cost to Use Plan

Operating Procedures

What Have You and Your City Accomplished So Far?

Step 1, City/County Schedule A

Here Is What You and the City Made Happen!

Note Re: "Seed Money"

    For 10,000 People

    For 5,000 People

    For 1,000 People

Diagram of Step 1, City/County Schedule A

2 **Chapter Two** 13

Step 2, City/County Schedule B

Format of City/County Schedule B

Summary of Step 2, City/County Schedule B

Diagram of Step 2, City/County Schedule B

Part Two—Reciprocal Support Plan at the State Level

Part Three—Reciprocal Support Plan at the Federal Level

Preface

Once upon a time (about thirty years ago), there were 24 employees, most of whom needed an advance against their paychecks. Being chief financial officer of the corporation, I approved the advances—not the best decision I ever made. It wasn't just that it became an accounting nightmare, but even worse, the employees were taking mighty tiny paychecks home to the wife and kiddies.

In the midst of all this chaos, I reversed my decision—no more advances against paychecks. But the workers were disgruntled. They still wanted the flexibility of advances. So I devised a new system. I set up a "money pot," which I funded out of my own pocket. (Using corporate funds for this venture was out of the question.) The workers could then access some money when they needed it, but it would not diminish their paychecks. Withdrawals from the "money pot" were interest free, but with each withdrawal the employee was required to "put a little something" back into the pot—like a small security deposit. The security deposits, of course, belonged to the employees and, as it turned out, were the beginnings of "savings accounts" for them.

As the years went by, more and more withdrawals were made and repaid, causing the "savings accounts" to increase dramatically. The workers were happy, the wives were happy, and the kiddies got their clothes and toys.

In due time, attrition, moves, changes of employment, sicknesses, and deaths ultimately brought an end to a wonderful era. Looking back, I realize that it was this wonderful era that sowed the seeds of the "Reciprocal Support Plan," which is the subject matter of this book.

I wish to thank all of the participants who helped bring this about.

Introduction

This book will introduce you to a new and astounding world of financial activity. The unusual (and perhaps even radical) approach to the handling and disbursement of the people's money, as well as the city's money, is taken step-by-step in a new, clear, and exciting direction.

The purpose of this financial activity is to better the lives of citizens while making their cities more fiscally sound. Participation in this plan is voluntary. Cities help the people, and the people help the cities. The name of this plan is the "Reciprocal Support Plan." It is not complex. In fact, the plan is the epitome of simplicity.

As the Reciprocal Support Plan progresses, citizens are able to make withdrawals at no interest from a city fund, but are required to put a small security deposit back into the city "pot." This deposit remains as a credit to the resident and is the beginning of a "savings account." The city meanwhile accumulates more usable revenue without increasing taxes or cutting entitlements. This ultimately leads to a financially healthy city, which provides all the services and protection the residents need and want.

After describing the basic plan, this book then goes on to the state level and shows how the state and its cities can work the Reciprocal Support Plan between themselves to the great advantage of both, such as using it to fund pension plans. Finally, the book goes on to the federal level and shows how the federal and state governments can work together to implement the Reciprocal Support Plan, which will help keep programs such as Social Security and Medicare solvent. In the overall view, the federal government is helping the states; the state governments are helping their cities and counties; and they, in turn, are helping the people, who are the ultimate and greatest beneficiaries of all.

PART ONE

Reciprocal Support Plan at the City/County Level

The Reciprocal Support Plan means...

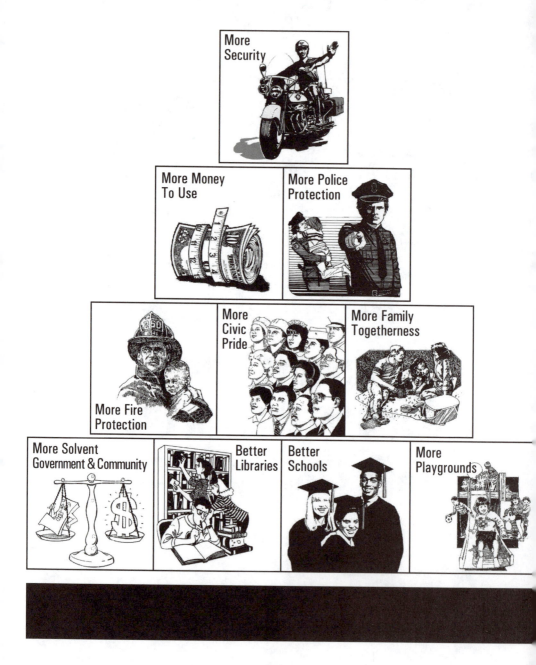

More
Security

More Money
To Use

More Police
Protection

More Fire
Protection

More
Civic
Pride

More Family
Togetherness

More Solvent
Government & Community

Better
Libraries

Better
Schools

More
Playgrounds

1

CHAPTER ONE

The Reciprocal Support Plan is an easy-to-follow, step-by-step guide to improving your life and that of your community. It will give you more security, more money, more police protection, more fire protection, more civic pride, more family togetherness, and a more solvent government and community. This is a plan that will create the best of living conditions for the people through the reciprocal support of their governments—city, county, state, and federal.

The plan needs your active involvement. Your help and the help of your neighbors is needed to convince your city to start up the Reciprocal Support Plan in your community. Without your urging, your city council will not know that you want the benefits this plan will give you. Your city council probably will not even know what benefits the Reciprocal Support Plan can bestow upon the city itself. You *must* make it clear to community leaders that the plan will increase the cash flow to the city so much that the city will be able to provide what the *residents* need and want.

Most people are eager to help their city and would do so happily—if only they knew what to do. This plan offers you a golden opportunity to do something definite, clear, and positive to better your city as well as your own life. All that needs to be done to get started is to arrange with your city leaders to set up the Reciprocal Support Plan for the residents of your city. Get together with your friends and neighbors. Take the city council out to lunch. Do whatever you have to do, but get the plan started in your city. It is vital to you and your family. You will be respected and admired for doing so.

Setting Up the Reciprocal Support Plan (RSP)

Setting up the plan is simple. You first find out which residents will voluntarily participate in it—homeowners, business owners, property owners, or any resident who is 18 years or older. The broader your base of participants, the better it is for the city. A person must be at least 18 years old and a legal resident of the city in order to participate. No other qualification is necessary. A husband and wife may each participate individually. In fact, any member of the family who is 18 years or older may participate individually. Your city attorney can draw up any legal papers needed to get started.

Refundable "seed money" is then allocated by the city, and the residents can begin making interest-free withdrawals according to the plan. Remember, this money is refundable. Any withdrawals immediately become "Accounts Payable" to the city. So the city's "Balance Sheet" remains the same, except that it increases by the amount of the security deposit paid in for the withdrawals. The withdrawals are paid back monthly to the city fund. Initially, the accounting and certifying of residents can be done by city employees. The plan calls for small service charges so that the costs will be covered.

No Cost to Use Plan

It doesn't cost a thing to use this plan. It is free of charge to the people and to the city. You won't need to buy anything or pay for anything to put the plan into motion. So get it moving as soon as possible. The residents and the city are the ones who will reap the profits.

Operating Procedures

The Reciprocal Support Plan will be controlled and operated by the city government. Step-by-step procedures are clearly outlined. The rules are simple and easy for anyone to follow. And, as more and more people participate in the plan, it will become evident that RSP is "the goose that laid the golden egg" for the people and their city.

The specific steps to proceed are as follows:

1. The city makes available to RSP, for each participant, an initial amount of $100.00 and succeeding increments of $100.00 as participants successfully complete each step of the plan.

2. Participants will withdraw from RSP the $100.00 at no interest and tax free and, simultaneously, pay to RSP a non-refundable 5% ($5.00) service charge and a *refundable* 15% ($15.00) security deposit, which goes directly into the city fund. The 5% service charge goes to the *RSP Service Division* to set up for the servicing of participants' accounts and for covering costs. The 15% security deposit, though it will not draw interest, remains as a *credit* to be used in good faith by RSP for the purposes of RSP. This is the beginning of a participant's savings. It is still the participant's money.

3. The participant redeposits the $100.00 with RSP over a period of four months at the rate of $25.00 per month. When the $100.00 has been redeposited fully, the use of it again becomes available to the participant, now with $100.00 additional credit to the participant's previous

credit of $15.00, totaling a $115.00 credit limit. But, hold on; this is just the beginning. The participant's credit limit will increase incredibly with each step of the plan.

4. RSP may regulate the rate of withdrawals by participants depending on the rate of cash flow and the amount of funds in the program at any time.

What Have You and Your City Accomplished So Far?

At this early stage, just four months into the program, if 10,000 people had participated simultaneously, RSP would have received $50,000.00 in service charges and an additional $150,000.00 in security deposits, which would have gone directly into the city fund, plus $1,000,000.00 in redeposited withdrawals. (See City/County Schedule A.)

Step 1, City/County Schedule A

There are eleven columns in city/county schedule A.

Column 1.	Shows the transaction date.
Column 2.	Shows the $100.00 advance made by the city to RSP.
Column 3.	Shows the $100.00 withdrawal made from RSP by the participant.
Column 4.	Shows the 5% service charge paid by participant at the time of withdrawal.
Column 5.	Shows the 15% security deposit paid by participant at the time of withdrawal.

Column 6.   Shows the redeposit by participant of the withdrawal over a period of four months at $25.00 per month.

Column 7.   Shows the outstanding withdrawal of $100.00 decreasing to zero as participant redeposits on a monthly basis.

Column 8.   Shows the cash balance of $15.00, which is the security deposit paid by participant. The cash balance increases as participant redeposits on a monthly basis. When participant has successfully completed the redeposit of $100.00, the cash balance will be $115.00. (Only then will the usage of the $115.00 be again available to participant.)

Column 9/10. Show the accumulated service charges and security deposits respectively, both of which will increase as participant completes each succeeding step in RSP. The security deposits are the "savings accounts" for the residents.

Column 11.   Shows the risk to which the city government is exposed, beginning with a minus $80.00. (This is the initial $100.00 advanced per participant, less the 5% and the 15% respectively for the service charge and security deposit.) The exposure diminishes as redeposits are made, ending at a positive $20.00.

Here Is What You and the City Made Happen!

After four months, the totals with 10,000, 5,000, and 1,000 people are shown at the bottom of City/County Schedule A.

Column 2.	City advances to RSP of $1 million (less recurrent redeposits; see following note).
Column 3.	New withdrawals from RSP of $1 million.
Column 4.	Service charges paid of $50,000.00.
Column 5.	Security deposits paid of $150,000.00.
Column 6.	Total redeposits of $1 million.
Column 7.	No withdrawals outstanding.
Column 8.	Cash balance of $1,150,000.00.
Column 9.	Service charges accumulated to $50,000.00.
Column 10.	Security deposits accumulated to $150,000.00.
Column 11.	*No* city exposure—*surplus* of $200,000.00 (less servicing costs).

Note Re: "Seed Money"

The figures at the bottom of column 2, Schedule A, showing city advances of $1 million, though accurate, are not the actual "seed money" needed from the city. Here's why: It is highly unlikely that 10,000 people will withdraw their first $100.00 at the exact same time. So let's assume that there would be 2,500 withdrawals per month over a period of four months, making a total of 10,000 withdrawals. With the same ratio applied to 5,000 people and 1,000 people, the cash requirements would then be as follows:

10

For 10,000 People

City advance	New wthdrl.	Less 5% serv.	Less 15% sec. dep.	Less redep.	Actual cash
$250,000	$250,000	-$12,500	-$37,500	0 =	$200,000
$250,000	$250,000	-$12,500	-$37,500	$62,500 =	$137,500
$250,000	$250,000	-$12,500	-$37,500	$125,000 =	$75,000
$250,000	$250,000	-$12,500	-$37,500	$187,500 =	$12,500

Instead of $1 million, the total cash needed for 10,000 people = $425,000

For 5,000 People

$125,000	$125,000	-$6,250	-$18,750	0 =	$100,000
$125,000	$125,000	-$6,250	-$18,750	-$31,250 =	$68,750
$125,000	$125,000	-$6,250	-$18,750	-$62,500 =	$37,500
$125,000	$125,000	-$6,250	-$18,750	-$93,750 =	$6,250

Instead of $500,000, the total cash needed for 5000 people = $212,500

For 1,000 People

$25,000	$25,000	-$1,250	-$3,750	0 =	$20,000
$25,000	$25,000	-$1,250	-$3,750	-6,250 =	$13,750
$25,000	$25,000	-$1,250	-$3,750	-$12,500 =	$7,500
$25,000	$25,000	-$1,250	-$3,750	-$18,750 =	$1,250

Instead of $100,000, the total cash needed for 1,000 people = $42,500

Now, let's see how the next step can get you more money to use at no interest.

Diagram of Step 1, City/County Schedule A

Name

1 Date	2 City/County Advance	3 New Withdrawal	4 Service Charge	5 Security Deposit	6 Redeposit Withdrawal	7 Outstanding Withdrawals	8 Cash Balance	9 Accumulated Service Chg.	10 Accumulated Security Dep.	11 City/County Exposure
Jan	$100.00	$100.00	$5.00	$15.00		$100.00	$15.00	$5.00	$15.00	-$80.00
Feb					$25.00	$75.00	$40.00			-$55.00
Mar					$25.00	$50.00	$65.00			-$30.00
Apr					$25.00	$25.00	$90.00			-$5.00
May					$25.00	0	$115.00			+$20.00
TOTALS for 10,000 people	$1million	$1 million	$50,000	$150,000	$1 million	0	$1,150,000	$50,000	$150,000	+$200,000
5,000 people	$500,000	$500,000	$25,000	$75,000	$500,000	0	$575,000	$25,000	$75,000	+$100,000
1,000 people	$100,000	$100,000	$5,000	$15,000	$100,000	0	$115,000	$5,000	$15,000	+$20,000

12

CHAPTER TWO

Step 2, City/County Schedule B

When citizens have successfully completed the first step, they can, at their convenience, proceed to Step 2. In Step 2, one can make a withdrawal of any amount up to the cash balance of one's cash account, namely $115.00, *plus* an additional bonus of $100.00 above the initial cash balance for having completed Step 1, totaling a $215.00 withdrawal. Again, the 5% service charge and the 15% security deposit would be paid by the participant. The monthly redeposits would now be spread over a period of five months. (See Diagram of Step 2, City/County Schedule B.)

Format of City/County Schedule B

The format of City/County Schedule B is identical to that of City/County Schedule A. Of course, the numbers in the columns change.

Column 2.	Another city advance of $100.00.
Column 3.	New withdrawal by participant of $215.00.
Column 4.	Service charge paid by participant of $10.75 (5%).

Column 5.	Security deposit paid by participant of $32.25 (15%).
Column 6.	Redeposit of withdrawal now spread over a period of five months at $43.00 per month.
Column 7.	Decreasing balance of withdrawal as monthly redeposits are made.
Column 8.	Increasing cash balance as participant makes monthly redeposits.
Column 9.	Service charges paid by participant in Schedules A and B have now accumulated to a total of $15.75.
Column 10.	Security deposits paid by participant in Schedules A and B have now accumulated to a total of $47.25.
Column 11.	Beginning city exposure of -$152.00 (which is the $200.00 total of two city advances less the $32.25 security deposit and less the $15.75 accumulated service charges). Also shown is the decreasing city exposure as monthly redeposits are made, ending with a surplus of $63.00.

Summary of Step 2, City/County Schedule B

It's amazing how much progress is being made. At the bottom of City/County Schedule B are totals for 10,000, 5,000, and 1,000 participants after completing Step 2.

Column 2.   City advances totaling $1 million (less recurrent redeposits).

Column 3.   New withdrawals from RSP of $2,150,000.00 drawn from the existing $1,150,000.00 cash balance plus the new city advance of $1,000,000.00.

Column 4.   Service charges paid in by the participants of $107,500.00.

Column 5.   Security deposits paid in by the participants of $322,500.00.

Column 6.   Total redeposits to RSP of $2,150,000.00.

Column 7.   No withdrawals outstanding.

Column 8.   Cash balances have increased to $2,472,500.00.

Column 9.   Service charges have now accumulated to $157,500.00.

Column 10.   Security deposits have now accumulated to $472,500.00.

Column 11.   No city exposure. *Surplus* is now $630,000.00 (less servicing costs).

These good results are bringing co-operation and trust between the people and the city. It all started with you and your efforts to get your city moving on this plan. You are encouraging the city to reach its potential, and the people of the city will like it.

Diagram of Step 2, City/County Schedule B

Name_____

1 Date	2 City/County Advance	3 New Withdrawal	4 Service Charge	5 Security Deposit	6 Redeposit Withdrawal	7 Outstanding Withdrawals	8 Cash Balance	9 Accumulated Service Chg.	10 Accumulated Security Dep.	11 City/County Exposure
May	$100.00	$215.00	$10.75	$32.25		$215.00	$32.25	$15.75	$47.25	-$152.00
Jun					$43.00	$172.00	$75.25			-$109.00
Jul					$43.00	$129.00	$118.25			-$66.00
Aug					$43.00	$86.00	$161.25			-$23.00
Sep					$43.00	$43.00	$204.25			+$20.00
Oct					$43.00	0	$247.25			+$63.00
TOTALS for 10,000 people	$1 million	$2.15 million	$107,500	$322,500	$2.15 million	0	$2,472,500	$157,500	$472,500	+$630,000
5,000 people	$500,000	$1,075,000	$53,750	$161,250	$1,075,000	0	$1,236,250	$78,750	$236,250	+$315,000
1,000 people	$100,000	$215,000	$10,750	$32,250	$215,000	0	$247,250	$15,750	$47,250	+$63,000

CHAPTER THREE

Step 3, City/County Schedule C

Those participants who have progressed through Steps 1 and 2 may now take Step 3. Participant's cash balance at this point is $247.25, so the next withdrawal from RSP may now be any amount up to $247.00 (leaving the 25 cents in the cash account) plus another additional bonus of $100.00 above the cash balance for having successfully completed Steps 1 and 2. (See Diagram of Step 3, City/County Schedule C for details.)

Format of Step 3, City/County Schedule C

Schedule C shows the usual service charges, security deposits, and redeposits required.

Column 2.	City advance to RSP of $100.00.
Column 3.	New withdrawal of $347.00.
Column 4.	Service charge of $17.35.
Column 5.	Security deposit of $52.05.
Column 6.	Redeposit of withdrawal in a period of five months at $69.40 per month.
Column 7.	Decreasing balance of withdrawal with monthly redeposits.

Column 8.	Increasing cash balance as redeposits are made up to $399.30.
Column 9.	Service charges paid in three Schedules (A, B, and C) have now accumulated a total of $33.10.
Column 10.	Security deposits paid in three Schedules (A, B, and C) have now accumulated a total of $99.30.
Column 11.	Decreasing city exposure from -$214.60 to a $132.40 *surplus*.

Summary of Step 3, City/County Schedule C

Theoretically, after one year and three months, you, your city, and RSP have brought into existence the following set of circumstances, as seen at the bottom of Schedule C:

1. RSP has now received $331,000.00 in service charges (column 9) with which to pay for new jobs servicing the residents' accounts with RSP and to cover operational costs.

2. The city government, which has thus far advanced a *net* of $1,676,000.00, is nevertheless on the positive side of the ledger with a *surplus* of $1,324,000.00 by virtue of the redeposits made by participants (column 11).

3. The people who have participated in the *Reciprocal Support Plan* have, at this point, already accumulated a credit line of $3,993,000.00 in their collective accounts (column 8). Furthermore, they have circulated $6,620,000.00, the total of their withdrawals, through the economy and back again to the *city*.

All of This Happened in Only 1 Year and 3 Months! (Theoretically)

To get these benefits coming to your city and its residents, you can arrange to have town hall and neighborhood meetings so that people can talk about the Reciprocal Support Plan and the benefits it brings. Better yet, phone your city council members and invite them to your home. Tell them you're having a "coffee klatch" and serving coffee and doughnuts or sweet rolls. Let them know your neighbors will be there. The city council members will be eager to attend because neighbors represent votes and council members campaigned to be elected in order to do some good for the city and its residents. Council members want to know what the people want. And an informal "coffee klatch" is just the place to find out.

During the meeting, let the council members know that you want the Reciprocal Support Plan started in your city. Explain to them what RSP does for the people, but also what it does for the city. Show them a couple of diagrams and schedules in the Reciprocal Support Plan book. Point out how the benefits increase with each step of the plan. Show them how the city comes out with a surplus of cash after each step of the plan. Tell them again and again that you and your neighbors want to get going on the plan in your city.

Some city council members might ask if anything like this plan has ever been tried before. So tell them about

Muhammad Yunus and the Grameen Bank in Bangladesh, whose financial plan has several similarities to the Reciprocal Support Plan (more on this later). For instance, they make small loans with easy repayments, they charge no interest on small loans, and they require no collateral. Starting with $27.00, the Grameen Bank now has millions of borrowers and hundreds of bank branches scattered over five continents. Grameen is in the banking business, but with many differences from traditional banks. Reciprocal Support Plan is *not* in the banking business, but it gives you additional benefits, which go far beyond what traditional banks can offer.

RSP—A Secondary Money System

If you are like most people, your primary sources of money are your salary and investments, along with banks, savings and loans, and credit card companies. The Reciprocal Support Plan creates a secondary flow of money for you. It's a backup for your existing income. You can get more money when you want it. And it's interest free!

This new, secondary money system lets you *use* more money and then return it. It's like using your neighbor's lawn mower and then returning it—or borrowing a cup of sugar and returning it. Good neighbors help each other.

The same goes for your city. You *use* the city's money, and the city *uses* yours and returns it. You help each other. This money system flows freely and independently between the city and its residents. It is self-sustaining.

There is no other plan in existence that will do what this plan will do. It's like walking into a new, wide-open world of economic freedom with lots of breathing space and lots of elbow room. You are free to withdraw money if you choose. You are free to increase your withdrawals with each step of

the plan. You are free to withdraw against your security deposits and still keep your entire "savings account." And, as
you make redeposits, you are free to take every nickel of your
payment off the balance. No interest is taken off—that's freedom! That's neighborly.

In the meantime, there is so much money pouring into
the city, there is no need to increase taxes or to cut entitlements. There is even enough money to help back up the city
pension plan. In short, the city is getting what it needs to do
its job. Because of your efforts to get the city moving on RSP,
you've made the world a better place. It all started with you!
The people will thank you and admire you for your insight.

Diagram of Step 3, City/County Schedule C

Name _____

1 Date	2 City/County Advance	3 New Withdrawal	4 Service Charge	5 Security Deposit	6 Redeposit Withdrawal	7 Outstanding Withdrawals	8 Cash Balance	9 Accumulated Service Chg.	10 Accumulated Security Dep.	11 City/County Exposure
Oct	$100.00	$347.00	$17.35	$52.05		$347.00	$52.30	$33.10	$99.30	-$214.60
Nov					$69.40	$277.60	$121.70			-$145.20
Dec					$69.40	$208.20	$191.10			-$75.80
YEAR 2										
Jan					$69.40	$138.80	$260.50			-$6.40
Feb					$69.40	$69.40	$329.90			+$63.00
Mar					$69.40	0	$399.30			+$132.40
TOTALS for										
10,000 people										
$1million	$3,470,000	$173,500	$520,500	$3,470,000	0	$3,993,000	$331,000	$993,000	+$1,324,000
5,000 people										
$500,000	$1,735,000	$86,750	$260,250	$1,735,000	0	$1,996,500	$165,500	$496,500	+$662,000
1,000 people										
$100,000	$347,000	$17,350	$52,050	$347,000	0	$399,300	$33,100	$99,300	+$132,400

CHAPTER FOUR

Steps 4 through 13, City/County Schedule D

Ｗhat follows from Steps 4 through 13 is shown in Schedule D. Each step follows the same pattern as the first three steps (Schedules A, B, and C), although in Schedule D, the redeposit dates are left blank for reasons of simplicity. As is evident, the numbers increase dramatically with each successive step, until Step 13 shows as follows:

Column 2.   The usual city advance to RSP of $100.00.

Column 3.   New withdrawal of $3,434.00. (Remember, this is *interest free!*)

Column 4.   Service charge of $171.70.

Column 5.   Security deposit of $515.10.

Column 6.   Monthly redeposits are left open, although the total redeposits in the amount of $3,434.00. is shown.

Column 7.   Decreasing balance of the withdrawal is not shown, but with redeposits, the balance goes down to zero.

Column 8.   Monthly increases in the cash balance are not shown, but with redeposits, the cash balance reaches $3,949.30.

Column 9. Service charges have now accumulated to $883.10.

Column 10. Security deposits have now accumulated to $2,649.30.

Column 11. This column hails a milestone in that city exposure reaches its highest peak of -$342.80 at the beginning of Step 7. In Step 8, the city exposure decreases for the first time and continues to decrease with each step thereafter until, for the first time, *city exposure is totally positive.* In Step 13, it starts with a surplus of $98.40 and ends, after redeposits, with a surplus of $3,532.40. Your city will *never again* be faced with a negative exposure in this program.

It bears repeating. In order for these good things to happen, the Reciprocal Support Plan needs to be set up in your city. You have to convince your city leaders to do it. This is your opportunity. Make it happen.

In order for you to get the full benefit of what's coming, you should be aware of the following possibilities:

1. You may withdraw money from your city through RSP at no interest.

2. You may use the money any way you see fit, including paying down credit cards with high interest rates.

3. You will start your own individual "savings account" with the security deposits you pay in with each withdrawal you make.

4. The total amount of your payment (redeposit) will come off the principal balance. No interest is charged.

5. Your total redeposits will be added to your paid-in security deposits to build up your credit line.

6. You will increase your city's revenues as you proceed step-by-step with the Reciprocal Support Plan (RSP).

Just imagine making all of this possible for your neighbors and friends. Imagine your city having enough money to give its residents all they need and want—thanks to you! Imagine it and you can make it happen. As Albert Einstein said, "Imagination is your preview of life's coming attractions." You have purpose. Make it good!

Diagram of Steps 4 through 13, City/County Schedule D

Name_____

1 Date	2 City/County Advance	3 New Withdrawal	4 Service Charge	5 Security Deposit	6 Redeposit Withdrawal	7 Outstanding Withdrawals	8 Cash Balance	9 Accumulated Service Chg.	10 Accumulated Security Dep.	11 City/County Exposure
Step 4	$100	$499	$24.95	$74.85		$499	$75.15	$58.05	$174.15	-$266.80
					$499	0	$574.15			+$232.20
Step 5	$100	$674	$33.70	$101.00		$674	$101.25	$91.75	$275.25	-$307.00
					$674	0	$775.25			+$367.00
Step 6	$100	$875	$43.75	$131.25		$875	$131.50	$135.50	$406.50	-$333.00
					$875	0	$1,006.50			+$542.00
Step 7	$100	$1,106	$55.30	$165.90		$1,106	$166.40	$190.80	$572.40	-$342.80
					$1,106	0	$1,272.40			+$763.20
Step 8	$100	$1,372	$68.60	$205.80		$1,372	$206.20	$259.40	$778.20	-$334.40
					$1,372	0	$1,578.20			+$1,037.60
Step 9	$100	$1,678	$83.90	$251.70		$1,678	$251.90	$343.30	$1,029.90	-$304.80
					$1,678	0	$1,929.90			+$1,373.20
Step 10	$100	$2,029	$101.45	$304.35		$2,029	$305.25	$444.75	$1,334.25	-$250.00
					$2,029	0	$2,334.25			+$1,779.00
Step 11	$100	$2,434	$121.70	$365.10		$2,434	$365.35	$566.45	$1,699.35	-$168.20
					$2,434	0	$2,799.35			+$2,265.80

Step 12	$100	$2,899	$144.95	$434.85		$2,899	$435.20	$711.40	$2,134.20	-$53.40
					$2,899	0	$3,334.20			+$2,845.60
Step 13	$100	$3,434	$171.70	$515.10		$3,434	$515.30	$883.10	$2,649.30	+$98.40
					$3,434	0	$3,949.30			+$3,532.40

TOTALS for Step 13

10,000 people

$1 mil	$34.34 mil	$1.717 mil	$5.151 mil	$34.34 mil	0	$39.493 mil	$8.831 mil	$26.493 mil	+$35.324 mil

5,000 people

$500,000	$17.17 mil	$858,500	$2.5755 mil	$17.17 mil	0	$19.746 mil	$4.4155 mil	$132465 mil	+$17.662 mil

1,000 people

$100,000	$3.434 mil	$171,700	$515,100	$3.434 mil	0	$3.9493 mil	$883,100	$2.6493 mil	+$3.5324mil

27

A Bit of History

Reciprocal Support Plan was first started in 1975 at a manufacturing firm in North Hollywood, California. Its purpose then was to provide interim loans to employees who needed cash between paychecks. The program ran successfully for almost thirty years, at which time it was discontinued.

Another financial plan with several similarities to Reciprocal Support Plan was started by Muhammad Yunus, a professor of economics at Chittagong University in Bangladesh. Professor Muhammad Yunus is known worldwide as the "Banker to the Poor." Following is a copy of an article put out recently by the Associated Press.

Microcredit: Inexpensive revolution for the poor

by Beth Duff-Brown
THE ASSOCIATED PRESS

DHAKA, Bangladesh—The father of a banking revolution that has helped millions of poor people says his "eureka moment" came while chatting to a shy woman weaving bamboo stools with calloused fingers.

Sufia Begum was a 21-year-old villager and a mother of three when economics professor Muhammad Yunus met her in 1974 and asked her how much she earned.

She said she borrowed 5 taka, about 9 cents, from a middleman for the bamboo for each stool.

All but two cents of that went back to the lender.

"I thought to myself, my God, for five takas she has become a slave," Yunus said.

That epiphany ultimately let to something called microcredit and the Grameen Bank, which has granted $4.18 billion in small loans to 3.12 million Bangladeshis. A model for microcredit financing in 65 developing countries, the system has helped some 17 million borrowers worldwide and pledges to eventually lift 100 million people from poverty.

In essence, one man from one isolated and blighted

country helped millions with just $27.

Not everyone sees microcredit as an unalloyed success story. Some economists both at home and abroad think the 99 percent loan recovery rate is an exaggeration, and complain Grameen's interest rates are too high.

Still, when more than 1,000 microcredit proponents recently gathered in Dhaka, the Bangladesh capital, to take stock of the movement, the star attraction was Yunus, the man Bill Clinton once said deserved a Nobel Prize.

Queen Sofia of Spain, honorary chairwoman of the Washington-based Microcredit Summit Campaign, called Yunus the "pioneer of this great and already universal achievement."

Not everyone is so taken with Yunus or his bank.

The critical economists say that small loans get vulnerable women hooked on credit and that the system does little to eradicate poverty.

"Microcredit has many flaws," said M.M. Akash, an economics professor at Dhaka University. It does not reach the extreme poor, who account for 20 percent of the population, he said. They have no homestead or land to cultivate and fear banking and investment. "It's a low-level poverty equilibrium trap."

Grameen does not require borrowers to have collateral. But the interest rates can run from zero for beggars—what Grameen calls "struggling members"—to 5 percent on a student loan and 20 percent for an income-generating loan to a small business.

Yunus said that's the price one pays to run Grameen free of donor debt from the Big Brothers of globalization, such as the World Bank. Aside from the 7 percent of the bank owned by the government, the borrowers of Grameen own all the equity.

He said poor women getting addicted to credit to improve their families' lives is no different from rich men obsessing over their stocks and bonds.

The critics, he said, typically do little to help the poor themselves, but are the first to claim that globalization will eliminate the ills of the world.

"Globalization is nobody's conspiracy. It's the order of the day," Yunus said. "But if you want to take it in the right direction, you must get the poor involved so the rich don't monopolize it."

Yunus believes there should be a body that monitors and regulates globalization, similar to what the United Nations does for world order and security.

What Is Microcredit?

In January of 2003, Muhammad Yunus published an article on the Internet titled "What Is Microcredit?" In this article, Professor Muhammad Yunus refers to Microcredit as "Grameencredit," named after his bank, Grameen Bank. The article explains that general features of Grameencredit are:

a) It promotes credit as a human right.

b) Its mission is to help poor families overcome poverty. It is targeted to help the poor, particularly poor women.

c) The most distinctive feature of Grameencredit is that it is not based on any collateral or legally enforceable contracts. It is based on "trust," not on legal procedures and system.

d) It is offered for creating self-employment for income-generating activities and housing for the poor, as opposed to consumption.

e) It was initiated as a challenge to conventional banking, which rejected the poor by classifying them as "not creditworthy." As a result, it rejected the basic methodology of conventional banking and created its own methodology.

f) It provides service at the doorstep of the poor based on the principle that the people should not go to the bank; the bank should go to the people.

g) In order to obtain loans a borrower must join a group of borrowers.

h) Loans can be received in a continuous sequence. New loans becomes available to a borrower if his or her previous loan is repaid.

i) All loans are to be paid back in installments (weekly or biweekly).

Even though the above features are not exactly identical to the Reciprocal Support Plan, there are many similarities, both actual and philosophical. Professor Muhammad Yunus, in his article, goes on to say:

Grameencredit is based on the premise that the poor have skills which remain unutilised or under-utilised. It is definitely not the lack of skills which make poor people poor. Grameen believes that the poverty is not created by the poor, it is created by the institutions and policies which surround them. In order to eliminate poverty all we need to do is to make appropriate changes in the institutions and policies, and/or create new ones. Grameen believes that charity is not an answer to poverty. It only helps poverty to continue. It creates dependency and takes away individual's initiative to break through the wall of poverty.

Grameen brought credit to the poor, women, the illiterate, the people who pleaded that they did not know how to invest money and earn an income. Grameen created a methodology and an institution around the financial needs of the poor, and created access to credit on a reasonable term enabling the poor to build on their existing skill to earn a better income in each cycle of loans.

For more information about Grameen, go to:
http://www.grameen-info.org/.

Trademarks and Copyright 1998 Grameen Communications; last modified on 22-December 2004.

CHAPTER FIVE

Frequently Asked Questions (FAQs)

Q. Is a $100.00 withdrawal too small as a first step?

A. No, it is not. Small is not ugly. "Small is beautiful." Small allows for more people to get involved. Many people could not handle *big* at the get-go. They need time to build up to it. However, for those people who would prefer larger withdrawals, Reciprocal Support Plan allows for faster repayment without prepayment penalties. This allows the participant to proceed faster through each step of the plan. And each step of the plan provides for a greater withdrawal, so that larger amounts are arrived at as quickly as the participant desires. For "big ticket" items, such as home mortgages, automobile loans, etc., people can apply to banks, savings and loans, or credit card companies.

Q. Since RSP has no late charges, wouldn't people tend to be tardy with their payments?

A. Not necessarily. If at all, it would only be a small percentage, since people want to pay their bills. They even enjoy it. They feel "right" about it. It maintains their dignity and pride. And they can hold up their heads in public. Furthermore, RSP is seen as a lifeline to a secondary income—interest free.

People do not want to run the risk of cutting off that lifeline by missing a payment or even being tardy with it. In addition, in the back of many people's minds is a vague apprehension of negative consequences if they default on a payment. People do pay back. Otherwise, banks, savings and loans, and credit card companies would close their doors and quit business. Instead, they keep begging to loan you more money.

Q. Where does the original money come from to fund withdrawals?

A. At the city/county level, the original advance money comes from the city or county in which the resident lives—probably from the general fund or the discretionary fund. Perhaps it would come $100.00 at a time as needed.

The initial $100.00 would first be shown as a "cash asset" on either of the governments' balance sheets. Then, immediately upon withdrawal, the $100.00 "cash asset" would be changed to an "accounts receivable" on the government balance sheet. In addition, the $15.00 security deposit paid by the participant upon withdrawal would show as a "cash asset." The balance sheet before and after the transaction would show as follows:

	Before	*After*
Cash assets	$100.00	$15.00
Accounts receivable	$0	$100.00
Total assets	$100.00	$115.00

Notice that the total assets on the city/county balance sheets increase with each transaction.

At the state level, the original withdrawal money is provided by the state to each of the cities and counties within its borders. At the federal level, the original withdrawal money

34

is provided by the federal government to each of the fifty states.

Q. How would RSP cope with fiscal irresponsibility, bureaucratic inefficiency, or outright corruption?

A. The simplicity of the components in RSP—that is, the withdrawal, service charge, security deposit, and the repayment—makes it so easy to follow and track that anyone can trace the flow of money. It would be difficult for either the citizens or the government to be fiscally irresponsible except by honest human error. Any flaw would show up quickly and could just as quickly be remedied.

As for inefficiency or corruption, RSP would just deal with it. That is, correct mistakes, call in law enforcement, track down criminals if any, and repair the damage as one would any natural disaster. These are not the fault of Reciprocal Support Plan, but they would be handled.

Other Operational Procedures

In Case of Default

What happens if a participant does not redeposit a withdrawal or is late with a payment?

1. Participant will still owe RSP the unpaid balance. (There are no late charges or prepayment penalties.)

2. Participant may not make any further withdrawals until the unpaid balance is paid in full.

3. Participant's cash balance account will belong to RSP, which may take whatever action it deems best to ensure that the withdrawal is paid in full, at which time the cash balance (less collection costs, if any) will again be available for participant's use.

In Case of Death

If a participant dies or becomes incapacitated, the participant's estate may first bring the account current or may pay it in full and then have it disbursed as outlined elsewhere herein.

Flexible Payments

The redeposit amounts shown in Schedules A, B, and C, etc. (as seen in column 6), are merely suggested amounts and, with *RSP approval*, are variable to suit the comfort of a participant's ability to make redeposits.

Even though a participant may elect, with *RSP approval*, his or her own redeposit schedule to suit personal cash-flow requirements, it would behoove *all* participants to make re-deposits as soon as possible, since this will build up cash balances *faster* and will entitle them to proceed to the next step *faster*, while, at the same time, making it possible to build city reserves *faster*, thus giving us all an expanded fire department, police department, etc., *faster!*

Voluntary Termination

Voluntary termination from RSP by participant is permissible under the following conditions:

1. Participant must have redeposited all of his or her withdrawals.

2. Participant may decide what portion, if any, of the credit balance he or she wishes to take out of RSP, the maximum being the full amount of the accumulated security deposits in the participant's account.

3. Disbursements out of participant's credit balance shall be made to participant on a pro-rata basis, factoring in the percentage of security deposits being taken out and the

number of months participant has had the use of withdrawal funds (at no interest). Such pro-rata portions of the credit balance shall be paid to participant monthly.

Voluntary Reentry

Voluntary reentry into RSP by participant may be accomplished by redepositing funds into his or her credit account at any level up to its previous high level. Participant may then begin again to make withdrawals. However, the extra $100.00 (bonus withdrawal) above the cash balance will not be made available until the cash balance level has reached its former highest level.

The *Reciprocal Support Plan* is designed to be flexible and accommodating to the volunteers participating in its success, yet very firm and resolved in achieving its purposes. Once the city debt is paid off and the budget deficit is under control, city officials may determine that the benefits engendered by RSP could also be achieved in myriad ways to enrich the lives of the people. Food, clothing, shelter, health care, education, communication, science, and, particularly, *the arts*, are just a few directions in which to pursue and to attain *"the good life."*

PART TWO

Reciprocal
Support Plan at the
State Level

CHAPTER SIX

The State Level

Now that we have seen what the city can do for its people (thanks to your hard work, perseverance, and encouragement), let's see what the state can do for its cities. Many of the fifty states are plagued by incessant budget deficits. They struggle very conscientiously to get out of the hole, but keep getting deeper and deeper into debt.

Arnold Schwarzenegger, Governor of California, came up against similar problems when he first came into office. He has since made several sweeping changes, which, one hopes, will bring a balanced budget to California.

Here's where the Reciprocal Support Plan comes to the rescue. Each state can get together with its cities and counties and get the plan started. The increase in cash flow to the state would be amazing, as seen in the following few steps at the state level. Simultaneously, cities and counties would benefit in huge ways. They all would come out ahead with huge amounts of money.

The state can set up RSP for its cities and counties in an almost identical manner as the city did for the people. However, whereas the city has thousands of residents as participants, the state only has the limited number of cities and counties within its borders as participants. California, for instance, contains about 477 cities.

In the following Schedules, we will see how the cash flow increases for both the state and the cities. Of course, this means greater advantages for the residents of all cities and counties. The fact that the state recognizes and appreciates what the cities and counties are doing for their people motivates the state to give its cities and counties a helping hand. Besides, the state benefits greatly from what's going on and will benefit even more by giving advances to its cities and counties because it will also increase the state's revenue.

Step 1, State Schedule A

Nine columns are used in the State Schedule A. The participant, either a city or a county, is named in the upper left corner of the page.

Column 1.　Shows the transaction date.

Column 2.　Shows the $100,000.00 advance made by the state to RSP. This is an arbitrary amount selected for the State of California. The amount of an advance will probably vary depending on how many cities and counties are in any particular state.

Column 3.　Shows the $100,000.00 withdrawal made by the city or county. Note: In previous Schedules, a 5% service charge was included, but, on the state level, there are so relatively few participants (just cities and counties) that the state can absorb the accounting costs.

Column 5.   Shows the security deposit of $15,000.00 (15%) made by the city or county participant.

Column 6.   Shows the redeposit of $25,000.00 per month for four months.

Column 7.   Shows the outstanding balance going down to zero.

Column 8.   Shows the cash balance of $15,000.00 growing to $115,000.00 as redeposits are made.

Column 10. Shows the accumulated security deposits.

Column 11. Shows the state exposure starting at - $85,000.00, which is the $100,000.00 advanced by the state, less the $15,000.00 security deposit put up by the participant. The state stands with a $15,000.00 surplus after the redeposits are made.

Summary of Step 1, State Schedule A

At the bottom of the State Schedule A, with 477 cities and counties participating in California, the totals are as follows:

Column 2. $47.7 million advanced to RSP from the state. (Again, bear in mind, the *actual* amount advanced in the first four months is only $22.8 million after security deposits and recurrent redeposits.)

Column 3.	$47.7 million withdrawn by 477 cities and/or counties.
Column 5.	$7.155 million security deposits put up by 477 cities or counties.
Column 6.	$47.7 million redeposited by cities or counties.
Column 7.	No outstanding withdrawals after redeposits.
Column 8.	$54.855 million cash balance in state fund.
Column 10.	$7.155 million accumulated security deposits.
Column 11.	No state exposure. In fact, there is a $7.155 million surplus.

How good can it get? In the meantime, the cities and counties have been funded to the point where they can provide even better services to their residents.

Diagram of Step 1, State Schedule A

Name_____

	2	3	4	5	6	7	8	9	10	11
1 Date	State Advance	New Withdrawal	Service Charge	Security Deposit	Redeposit Withdrawal	Outstanding Withdrawals	Cash Balance	Accumulated Service Chg.	Accumulated Security Dep.	State Exposure
Jan	$100,000	$100,000	0	$15,000		$100,000	$15,000	0	$15,000	-$85,000
Feb					$25,000	$75,000	$40,000			-$60,000
Mar					$25,000	$50,000	$65,000			-$35,000
Apr					$25,000	$25,000	$90,000			-$10,000
May					$25,000	0	$115,000			+$15,000

TOTALS for 477 cities

$47,700,000	$47,700,000	0	$7,155,000	$47,700,000	0	$54,855,000	0	$7,155,000	$7,155,000

CHAPTER SEVEN

Step 2, State Schedule B

I t keeps getting better. Step 2 at the state level brings even more benefits to the cities and counties as well as to the state itself.

The State Schedule B (Step 2) follows closely the State Schedule A. It also uses nine columns as follows:

Column 1.   Transaction date.

Column 2.   Additional $100,000.00 advance by state to RSP.

Column 3.   New withdrawal by city or county of $215,000.00, which includes previous credit of $115,000.00 plus a bonus of $100,000.00 for having completed state Step 1.

Column 5.   15% security deposit $32,250.00 paid by city or county.

Column 6.   This column shows the monthly redeposits of the withdrawal.

Column 7.   Shows decreasing outstanding withdrawal with each monthly redeposit.

Column 8.   Increasing state cash balance with each monthly redeposit.

Column 10. Accumulated security deposits of $47,250.00.

Column 11. Shows decreasing state exposure from - $167,750.00 to a positive $47,250.00. No state exposure.

Summary of Step 2, State Schedule B

The bottom of State Schedule B shows the totals for 477 California cities and/or counties after completing Step 2:

Column 2.   State advances of $47.7 million less recurring redeposits.

Column 3.   Total withdrawals by 477 cities or counties of $102,555,000.

Column 5.   15% security deposits equal $15,383,250.00.

Column 6.   Redeposits of $102,555,000.

Column 7.   Decreasing balance of withdrawals to zero.

Column 8.   Increasing state cash balance to $117,938,250.00.

Column 10. Total accumulated security deposits of $22,538,250.00.

Column 11. State exposure, which started at a negative, is now at a positive $22,538,250.00 with no state exposure.

Diagram of Step 2, State Schedule B

Name _____

	1 Date	2 State Advance	3 New Withdrawal	4 Service Charge	5 Security Deposit	6 Redeposit Withdrawal	7 Outstanding Withdrawals	8 Cash Balance	9 Accumulated Service Chg.	10 Accumulated Security Dep.	11 State Exposure
	May	$100,000	$215,000	0	$32,250		$215,000	$32,250	0	$47,250	$167,750
	Jun					$43,000	$172,000	$75,250			$124,750
	Jul					$43,000	$129,000	$118,250			$81,750
	Aug					$43,000	$86,000	$161,250			$38,750
	Sep					$43,000	$43,000	$204,250			+ $4,250
	Oct					$43,000	0	$247,250			+ $47,250

TOTALS for 477 cities

		$47,700,000	$102,555,000	0	$15,383,250	$102,555,000	0	$117,938,250	0	$22,538,250	$22,538,250

49

CHAPTER EIGHT

Step 3, State Schedule C

T he pot gets bigger. Step 3, State Schedule C keeps the cash flow growing as follows:

Column 1.   Transaction date.

Column 2.   Another state advance of $100,000.00.

Column 3.   New withdrawal of $347,000.00.

Column 5.   Security deposit of $52,050.00.

Column 6.   Redeposits of withdrawal.

Column 7.   Decreasing balance of withdrawal with monthly redeposits.

Column 8.   Increasing state cash balance with each monthly redeposit up to $399,300.00.

Column 10. Accumulated security deposits up to $99,300.00.

Column 11. No state exposure. Surplus of $99,300.00.

Summary of Step 3, State Schedule C

Totals for 477 cities and/or counties are shown at the bottom of State Schedule C:

Column 2.   State advances of $47,700,000.00.

Column 3.   Withdrawals of $165,519,000.00.

Column 5.   Security deposits of $24,827,850.00.

Column 6.   Redeposits of $165,519,000.00.

Column 7.   Outstanding withdrawals down to zero.

Column 8.   State cash balance up to $190,466,100.00.

Column 10. Accumulated security deposits of $47,366,100.00.

Column 11. No state exposure. Surplus of $47,366,100.00.

Diagram of Step 3, State Schedule C

Name _____

1 Date	2 State Advance	3 New Withdrawal	4 Service Charge	5 Security Deposit	6 Redeposit Withdrawal	7 Outstanding Withdrawals	8 Cash Balance	9 Accumulated Service Chg.	10 Accumulated Security Dep.	11 State Exposure
Oct	$100,000	$347,000	0	$52,050		$347,000	$52,300	0	$99,300	-$247,700
Nov					$69,400	$277,600	$121,700			-$178,300
Dec					$69,400	$208,200	$191,100			-$108,900
YEAR 2										
Jan					$69,400	$138,800	$260,500			-$39,500
Feb					$69,400	$69,400	$329,900			+$29,900
Mar					$69,400	0	$399,300			+$99,300

TOTALS for 477 cities

	$47,700,000	$165,519,000	0	$24,827,850	$165,519,000	0	$190,466,100	0	$47,366,100	+$47,366,100

CHAPTER NINE

Steps 4 through 13, State Schedule D

State Schedule D shows Steps 4 through 13 and sends the figures soaring. Step 13 reaches the following figures:

Column 2.	State advance of $100,000.00.
Column 3.	New withdrawal of $3,434,000.00.
Column 5.	Security deposit of $515,100.00.
Column 6.	Redeposits of $3,434,000.00.
Column 7.	Outstanding balance of withdrawals of zero.
Column 8.	State cash balance of $3,949,300.00.
Column 10.	Accumulated security deposits of $2,649,300.00.
Column 11.	No state exposure. Surplus of $2,649,300.00.

Summary of Step13, State Schedule D

At the bottom of State Schedule D, after Step 13, the totals for 477 California cities and/or counties are as follows:

Column 2.　State advances of $47,700,000.00.

Column 3.　Withdrawals of $1,638,018,000.00.

Column 5.　Security deposits of $245,702,700.00.

Column 6.　Redeposits of $1,638,018,000.00.

Column 7.　No outstanding withdrawals.

Column 8.　State cash balance of $1,883,816,100.00.

Column 10.　Accumulated security deposits of $1,263,716,100.00.

Column 11.　No state exposure. *Surplus* of $1,263,716,100.00.

Diagram of Steps 4 through 13, State Schedule D   Name_____

1 Date	2 State Advance	3 New Withdrawal	4 Service Charge	5 Security Deposit	6 Redeposit Withdrawal	7 Outstanding Withdrawals	8 Cash Balance	9 Accumulated Service Chg.	10 Accumulated Security Dep.	11 State Exposure
Step	$100,000	$499,000		$74,850		$499,000	$75,150	0	$174,150	-$324,850
4					$499,000	0	$574,150	0		+174,150
Step	$100,000	$674,000		$101,100		$674,000	$101,250		$275,250	-$398,750
5					$674,000	0	$775,250	0		+$275,250
Step	$100,000	$875,000		$131,250		$875,000	$131,500		$406,500	-$468,500
6					$875,000	0	$1,006,500	0		+$406,500
Step	$100,000	$1,106,000		$165,900		$1,106,000	$166,400		$572,400	-$533,600
7					$1,106,000	0	$1,272,400	0		+$572,400
Step	$100,000	$1,372,000		$205,800		$1,372,000	$206,200		$778,200	-$593,800
8					$1,372,000	0	$1,578,200	0		+$778,200
Step	$100,000	$1,678,000		$251,700		$1,678,000	$251,900		$1,029,900	-$648,100
9					$1,678,000	0	$1,929,900	0		+$1,029,900

(continued on next page)

57

Diagram of Steps 4 through 13, State Schedule D *(continued)*

1 Date	2 State Advance	3 New Withdrawal	4 Service Charge	5 Security Deposit	6 Redeposit Withdrawal	7 Outstanding Withdrawals	8 Cash Balance	9 Accumulated Service Chg.	10 Accumulated Security Dep.	11 State Exposure
Step	$100,000	$2,029,000		$304,350		$2,029,000	$305,250		$1,334,250	-$694,750
10					$2,029,000	0	$2,334,250	0		+$1,334,250
Step	$100,000	$2,434,000		$365,100		$2,434,000	$365,350		$1,699,350	-$734,650
11					$2,434,000	0	$2,799,350	0		+$1,699,350
Step	$100,000	$2,899,000		$434,850		$2,899,000	$435,200		$2,134,200	-$764,800
12					$2,899,000	0	$3,334,200	0		+$2,134,200
Step	$100,000	$3,434,000		$515,100		$3,434,000	$515,300		$2,649,300	-$784,700
13					$3,434,000	0	$3,949,300	0		+$2,649,300
TOTALS for 477 cities at Step 13	$47,700,000	$1,638,018,000		$245,702,700	$1,638,018,000		$1,883,816,100	0	$1,263,716,100	+$1,263,716,100

58

PART THREE

Reciprocal Support Plan at the Federal Level

CHAPTER TEN

The Federal Level

T he states will now be doing so well with their cities and counties and piling up so much positive surplus that the federal government will be eager to get in the act.

The Reciprocal Support Plan (RSP) can easily be set up for the federal government and the fifty states as participants. They can operate in the same manner as the states operate with their cities and as the cities operate with their residents. It all works. The system is mechanically beautiful, and it all benefits the people.

Step 1, Federal Schedule A

Nine columns are used in Federal Schedule A. One of the fifty states is named in the upper left of the page as the participant. Each state, of course, will have its own page.

Column 1.   Transaction date.

Column 2.   Shows a $25 million advance made by the federal government to RSP to be withdrawn by the named state. This amount of $25 million may vary depending on the population and needs of a particular state.

Column 3.	The state makes a withdrawal of $25 million.
Column 5.	A security deposit of $3,750,000.00 is paid by the state at time of withdrawal.
Column 6.	Shows the redeposit of $6,250,000.00 per month for four months made by the state.
Column 7.	Shows the outstanding balance of the withdrawal going to zero.
Column 8.	Shows the federal cash balance of $3,750,000.00 growing to $28,750,000.00 as redeposits are made.
Column 10.	Shows the accumulated security deposits, which will build up with each succeeding step of the plan.
Column 11.	Federal exposure begins at – $21,250,000.00, but soon builds up to a positive $3,750,000.00.

Summary of Step 1, Federal Schedule A

The totals with all fifty states participating are shown at the bottom of Federal Schedule A as follows:

Column 2.	$1,250,000,000.00 advanced to RSP by the federal government. (Remember, the ACTUAL amount advanced in the first four months is only $593,750,000.00 after security deposits and recurrent redeposits.)

Column 3. $1,250,000,000.00 withdrawn by fifty states.

Column 5.   Paid in security deposits of $187,500,000.00.

Column 6.   Redeposits of $1,250,000,000.00.

Column 7.   No outstanding withdrawals remaining.

Column 8.   Federal cash balance of $1,437,500,000.00.

Column 10. $187,500,000.00 accumulated security deposits.

Column 11. No federal exposure. Instead, there is a surplus of $187,500,000.00.

The federal government is now on a roll. Where it's headed is almost unbelievable. And the states are benefiting as well. Now, let's head for Step 2 in Federal Schedule B.

Diagram of Step 1, Federal Schedule A

Name _____

1 Date	2 Federal Advance	3 New Withdrawal	4 Service Charge	5 Security Deposit	6 Redeposit Withdrawal	7 Outstanding Withdrawals	8 Cash Balance	9 Accumulated Service Chg.	10 Accumulated Security Dep.	11 Federal Exposure
Jan	$25,000,000	$25,000,000	0	$3,750,000		$25,000,000	$3,750,000	0	$3,750,000	-$21,250,000
Feb					$6,250,000	$18,750,000	$10,000,000			-$15,000,000
Mar					$6,250,000	$12,500,000	$16,250,000			-$8,750,000
Apr					$6,250,000	$6,250,000	$22,500,000			-$2,500,000
May					$6,250,000	0	$28,750,000			+$3,750,000
TOTALS for 50 states	$1 billion, 250 million	$1,250,000,000		$187,500,000	$1 billion, 250million	0	$1,437,500,000	0	$187,500,000+$187,500,000	

11

CHAPTER ELEVEN

At this point, financial activity in the millions and even billions of dollars is reaping big surpluses for the federal government as well as for the fifty states. It can't be stressed enough how important it is for you to get the ball rolling by convincing your city to install the Reciprocal Support Plan. Even though it starts out with only $100.00 withdrawals, those withdrawals will eventually be up to $25 million made by the states and will get even bigger. And it all helps the people.

Step 2, Federal Schedule B

The same pattern is followed in the federal Step 2 as in the federal Step 1. The numbers change, of course, as follows:

Column 2.   Federal advance of $25 million.

Column 3.   State withdrawal of $53,750,000.00.

Column 5.   Security deposit of $8,062,500.00.

Column 6.   Monthly redeposits of $10,750,000.00 for a period of five months.

Column 7.   Shows outstanding withdrawals going to zero with redeposits.

Column 8. Federal cash balance of $8,062,500.00 increases to $61,812,500.00 as redeposits are made.

Column 10. Accumulated security deposits are now $11,812,500.00.

Column 11. Negative federal exposure of -$41,937,500.00 drops down to zero and then builds up to a positive surplus of $11,812,500.00.

Summary of Step 2, Federal Schedule B

The totals for federal Step 2, with all fifty states participating, are at the bottom of Federal Schedule B, as follows:

Column 2. Federal advance of $1,250,000,000.00 less recurrent redeposits and security deposits.

Column 3. Fifty state withdrawals totaling $2,687,500,000.00.

Column 4. Security deposits paid in by states of $403,125,000.00.

Column 5. Redeposits of withdrawals of $2,687,500,000.00.

Column 6. No remaining withdrawals outstanding.

Column 7. Federal cash balance of $3,090,625,000.00.

Column 8. Accumulated security deposits of $590,625,000.00.

Column 9. No federal exposure. There is now a federal surplus of $590,625,000.00.

Diagram of Step 2, Federal Schedule B

Name_____

1 Date	2 Federal Advance	3 New Withdrawal	4 Service Charge	5 Security Deposit	6 Redeposit Withdrawal	7 Outstanding Withdrawals	8 Cash Balance	9 Accumulated Service Chg.	10 Accumulated Security Dep.	11 Federal Exposure
May	$25,000,000	$53,750,000	0	$8,062,500		$53,750,000	$8,062,500	0	$11,812,500	-$41,937,500
Jun						$43,000,000	$18,812,500			-$31,187,500
Jul					$10,750,000	$32,250,000	$29,562,500			-$20,437,500
Aug					$10,750,000	$21,500,000	$40,312,500			-$9,687,500
Sep					$10,750,000	$10,750,000	$51,062,500			+$1,062,500
Oct					$10,750,000	0	$61,812,500			+$11,812,500

TOTALS for 50 states

	$1,250,000,000	$2,687,500,000	0	$403,125,000	$2,687,500,000	0	$3,090,625,000	0	$590,625,000	+$590,625,000

67

Surpluses Keep Adding Up!

CHAPTER TWELVE

Surpluses keep mounting for the federal government and the fifty states. Take a look at what's happening in federal Step 3.

Step 3, Federal Schedule C

It keeps on going. Again, the pattern is the same for federal Step 3 as for federal Steps 1 and 2, as follows:

Column 2.   Another federal advance of $25 million.

Column 3.   New withdrawal of $86,812,500.00.

Column 5.   Security deposit paid by state of $13,021,875.00.

Column 6.   Redeposit of withdrawal of $17,362,500.00 per month for five months.

Column 7.   Outstanding withdrawal goes down to zero with redeposits.

Column 8.   Federal cash balance starts at $13,021,875.00 and builds up to $99,834,375.00.

Column 10. Accumulated security deposits have built up to $24,834,375.00.

Column 11. Federal exposure of -$61,978,125.00 gets wiped out, and a positive surplus is built up to $24,834,375.00.

Summary of Step 3, Federal Schedule C

Totals are shown at the bottom of Federal Schedule C with fifty states participating in federal Step 3, as follows:

Column 2. Federal advance of $1,250,000,000.00.

Column 3. Total withdrawals by fifty states of $4,340,625,000.00.

Column 5. Paid in security deposits of $651,093,750.00.

Column 6. Redeposits of withdrawals add up to $4,340,625,000.00.

Column 7. There are no outstanding withdrawals.

Column 8. Federal cash balance is now up to $4,991,718,750.00.

Column 10. Accumulated security deposits of $1,241,718,750.00.

Column 11. No remaining federal exposure. The federal surplus is now $1,241,718,750.00.

That's a healthy surplus. It makes figuring out a budget a lot easier. Former Senator Everett Dirksen is often quoted as having said, in the middle of a budget meeting, "A billion here, a billion there; soon we'll be talking real *money*."

Diagram of Step 3, Federal Schedule C

RECIPROCAL SUPPORT PLAN

Name _____

1 Date	2 Federal Advance	3 New Withdrawal	4 Service Charge	5 Security Deposit	6 Redeposit Withdrawal	7 Outstanding Withdrawals	8 Cash Balance	9 Accumulated Service Chg.	10 Accumulated Security Dep.	11 Federal Exposure
Oct	$25,000,000,000	$86,812,500	0	$13,021,875		$86,812,500	$13,021,875	0	$24,834,375	-$61,978,125
Nov					$17,362,500	$69,450,000	$30,384,375			-$44,615,625
Dec					$17,362,500	$52,087,500	$47,746,875			-$27,253,125
YEAR 2										
0Jan					$17,362,500	$34,725,000	$65,109,375			-$9,890,625
Feb					$17,362,500	$17,362,500	$82,471,875			+$7,471,875
Mar					$17,362,500	0	$99,834,375			+$24,834,375
TOTALS for 50 states	$1,250,000,000			$651,093,750			$4,991,718,750	0		+$1,241,718,750
		$4,340,625,000				$4,340,625,000			$1,241,718,750	

72

13

CHAPTER THIRTEEN

Steps 4 through 13, Federal Schedule D

Federal Schedule D now takes us from federal Step 4 through federal Step 13. With fifty states participating, we are now into billions of dollars. As you can see, with everyone doing their part, the system works automatically. Each step of the way is another step up and all participants benefit.

Summary of Step 13, Federal Schedule D

Column 2.   Federal advance of $1,250,000,000.00.

Column 3.   New withdrawals by fifty states total $42,939,892,000.00.

Column 5.   Security deposits paid in by the states total $6,440,983,500.00.

Column 6.   Redeposits of withdrawals total $42,939,892,000.00.

Column 7.   No remaining outstanding withdrawals.

Column 8.   Federal cash balance of $49,380,875,000.00.

Column 10. Accumulated security deposits are now at $33,130,876,000.00.

Column 11. No federal exposure. Instead, there is a
federal surplus of $33,130,876,000.00.

Tip O'Neill, former speaker of the House of Representa-
tives, often said, "All politics are local." What you do locally
affects not only your own city and county, but all fifty states
and the federal government as well. As you progress with the
Reciprocal Support Plan in your city, the whole country is
watching. Everyone is interested. Everyone cares. Because
politics all boils down to the people. That's what's important.
How does all the politicking benefit the people everywhere?
What's in it for the people? That's what counts.

Yes! What counts are the benefits that go to the people.
Let's review what has happened from day one, when you
talked with your city leaders about the Reciprocal Support
Plan. You convinced them that RSP was a good plan, so they
got it started in your city. Then the residents began making
interest-free withdrawals. We followed the increasing amounts
of the withdrawals from $100.00 in Step 1, up to $3,434.00
in Step 13. Of course, the withdrawals would continue up-
wards as long as the participants were willing.

At the same time, your city began giving advances of
$100.00 to each participating resident and advanced an addi-
tional $100.00 with each step of the plan. We followed the
activity through Step 13. Even though the city gave advances
of $100.00 through 13 steps, totaling $1,300.00, the city had
a surplus of $3,532.40 after Step 13. That's for each resident
participating. For 10,000 residents, that comes to a
$35,324,000.00 surplus. With that kind of money, a lot of
benefits can be bestowed on the people. And that's not the
end of it. The benefits can continue so long as the participants are willing. You see how important you are to this whole
program.

Now we look at the state level. Here we see the states, which are floundering in debt, install RSP and increase their usable revenue by incredible amounts. Starting with state advances of $100,000.00 to each of its cities and/or counties, the state built up a cash balance of $3,949,300.00. With 477 cities and/or counties (as in California), that adds up to a cash balance of $1,883,816,100.00 for the state. In the meantime, the cities and counties are increasing their withdrawals from the state from $100,000.00 in state Step 1 to a mind-boggling $3,434,000.00 in state Step 13. That's for each and every city or county in the state. The people are now being given unheard-of benefits.

We finally look at the federal level. Here we see a critical need for the Reciprocal Support Plan. Why? Because our federal government presently owes a national debt of about seven trillion dollars and is still running a budget deficit. The seven trillion dollar national debt is costing us approximately one billion dollars each day in interest.

can be saved by RSP

Dollars for Medicare & healthcare benefits

Help for disaster victims

Furthermore, Social Security and Medicare are in deep trouble. The onrush of 78 million "Baby Boomers," those born between 1946 and 1964, beginning to reach retirement age in year 2008 at age 62 could very well inundate the Social Security System. The same goes for Medicare when the "Boomers" start qualifying for it in year 2011 at age 65.

Politicians as well as most economists agree that the Social Security and Medicare systems are facing horrific financial disaster, but no one has come up with a solution. The Reciprocal Support Plan, however, can help keep the two systems alive. The cash surpluses that RSP creates for the federal government can be used for that very purpose. The federal government can easily set up RSP with the fifty states participating. With federal advances of $25 million to each of the states in federal Step 1, the federal cash balance reaches $49,380,875,000.00 in federal Step 13 and will still continue upward as long as the participants wish.

Taking another overall view, the federal government is helping the states, the states are helping their cities and counties, and they, in turn, are helping the people, who are the ultimate and greatest beneficiaries of all.

Diagram of Steps 4 through 13, Federal Schedule D

Name _____

1 Date	2 Federal Advance	3 New Withdrawal	4 Service Charge	5 Security Deposit	6 Redeposit Withdrawal	7 Outstanding Withdrawals	8 Cash Balance	9 Accumulated Service Chg.	10 Accumulated Security Dep.	11 Federal Exposure
Step 4	$25,000,000	$124,834,375	0	$18,725,156		$124,834,375	$18,725,156	0	$43,559,531	-$81,274,850
					$124,834,375	0	$143,559,520			+ $43,559,520
Step 5	$25,000,000	$168,559,520	0	$25,283,928		$168,559,520	$25,283,928	0	$68,843,459	-$99,716,080
					$168,559,520	0	$193,843,440			+ $68,843,440
Step 6	$25,000,000	$218,843,440	0	$32,826,516		$218,843,440	$32,826,516	0	$101,669,970	-$117,173,490
					$218,843,440	0	$251,669,950			+ $101,669,950
Step 7	$25,000,000	$276,669,950	0	$41,500,492		$276,669,950	$41,500,492	0	$143,170,460	-$133,499,510
					$276,669,950	0	$318,170,440			+ $143,170,440
Step 8	$25,000,000	$343,170,440	0	$51,475,566		$343,170,440	$51,475,566	0	$194,646,020	-$148,524,440
					$343,170,440	0	$394,646,000			+ $194,646,000
Step 9	$25,000,000	$419,646,000	0	$62,946,900		$419,646,000	$62,946,900	0	$257,592,920	-$162,053,100
					$419,646,000	0	$482,592,900			+ $257,592,900

(continued on next page)

77

Diagram of Steps 4 through 13, Federal Schedule D *(continued)*

1 Date	2 Federal Advance	3 New Withdrawal	4 Service Charge	5 Security Deposit	6 Redeposit Withdrawal	7 Outstanding Withdrawals	8 Cash Balance	9 Accumulated Service Chg.	10 Accumulated Security Dep.	11 Federal Exposure
Step 10	$25,000,000	$507,592,900	0	$76,138,935		$507,592,900	$507,592,900	0	$333,731,850-$173,861,070	
					$507,592,900	0	$583,731,830			+$333,731,830
Step 11	$25,000,000	$608,731,830	0	$91,309,774		$608,731,830	$608,731,830	0	$425,041,620-$183,690,230	
					$608,731,830	0	$700,041,600			+$425,041,600
Step 12	$25,000,000	$725,041,600	0	$108,756,240		$725,041,600	$725,041,600	0	$533,797,860-$191,243,760	
					$725,041,600	0	$833,797,840			+$533,797,840
Step 13	$25,000,000	$858,797,840	0	$128,819,670		$858,797,840	$858,797,840	0	$662,617,530-$196,180,330	
					$858,797,840	0	$987,617,510			+$662,617,510
TOTALS for 50 states at Step 13	$1,250,000,000	$42,939,892,000	0	$6,440,983,500		0	$49,380,875,000	0	$33,130,876,000	
	$42,939,892,000				$42,939,892,000					+$33,130,876,000

78

Index

Give the Gift of

Reciprocal Support Plan

to Your Friends and Colleagues

CHECK YOUR LEADING BOOKSTORE OR ORDER HERE

❑ **YES**, I want _____ copies of *Reciprocal Support Plan* at $16.95 each, plus $4.95 shipping per book (Ohio and California residents please add $1.31 sales tax per book.) Canadian orders must be accompanied by a postal money order in U.S. funds. Allow 15 days for delivery.

My check or money order for $_____ is enclosed.

Please charge my: ❑ Visa ❑ MasterCard ❑ Discover ❑ American Express

Name _____

Organization _____

Address _____

City/State/Zip _____

Phone_____ Email_____

Card # _____

Exp. Date_____ Signature _____

Please make your check payable and return to:

BookMasters, Inc.
P.O. Box 388 • Ashland, OH 44805

Call your credit card order to (800) 247-6553
Fax (419) 281-6883

order@bookmasters.com   www.atlasbooks.com